SOUTH AFRICA SINCE 1948

Jean Hayward

Wayland

Titles in this series

The Arab–Israeli Conflict
China since 1945
The Cold War
The Origins of the First World War
The Russian Revolution
South Africa since 1948
The Third Reich
The United Nations

Cover illustration: Poster by End Conscription Campaign. Hector Peterson, the first child to be killed in the Soweto massacre.

First published in 1989 by
Wayland (Publishers) Ltd
61 Western Road, Hove
East Sussex BN3 1JD, England

Editor: Catherine Ellis
Designer: Ross George
Consultant: Dr Kevin Shillington, freelance historian and education consultant.

British Library Cataloguing in Publication Data
Hayward, Jean
  South Africa since 1948. – (Witness series).
  1. South Africa, 1948–
  I. Title   II. Series
  968.05

  ISBN 1–85210–438–4

Typeset by Kalligraphics Limited, Horley, Surrey
Printed and bound by Sagdos, S.p.A., Milan

Contents

Apartheid

SINCE JUNE 1976, when Sowetan students rose in revolt and were killed in clashes with armed forces, television news items about South Africa have often shown young black people confronting the police and army. Nearly a thousand children have been killed by police bullets, sometimes during demonstrations, sometimes on their way to school, sometimes even in the school playground. Once in detention children are often assaulted, beaten and tortured in order to try to force them to sign statements admitting guilt. Although their demonstrations were primarily aimed against the inferior education provided for blacks, the students also identified with the struggle for basic human rights.

Unrest amongst black people is widespread. In June 1986 the South African government declared a State of Emergency, allowing all sorts of restrictions to be imposed on thirty-six districts of the country. Among its more threatening effects, the State of Emergency gave the police greater powers to arrest and detain people, it banned public gatherings, including mass funerals outside, and it enforced press censorship. Media censorship now extends to foreign journalists: the reporting or filming of any activity connected with violence is forbidden. During the first five months of the State of Emergency nearly 9,000 children were detained in police cells and prisons. Many parents do not know whether their children are dead, in prison, or in hiding.

The conflict in South Africa is over its

In areas where the State of Emergency is in force, mass open-air funerals such as this one are banned by the government.

THE **WEEKLY MAIL**

PRICES:

Volume 2, Number 24, FRIDAY JUNE 20 to THURSDAY JUNE 26, 1986

THE PAPER FOR A CHANGING SOUTH AFRICA

WE'RE BACK ON THE STREETS!
The paper that was seized last week will be on sale as usual from today

| The EPG report: An extraordinary document made ordinary by our extraordinary laws. | **8** | A leaf-munching plan to beat malnutrition | **7** |

FRONT PAGE COMMENT

Our lawyers tell us we can say almost nothing critical about the Emergency

But we'll try:

P IK BOTHA, the Minister of Foreign Affairs, told US television audiences this week that the South African press remained free.
We hope that ▬▬▬▬▬▬▬▬▬▬▬▬▬ ▬▬▬▬▬▬, was listening.

They considered our publication subversive.
● If it is subversive to speak out against ▬▬▬▬▬, we plead guilty.
● If it is subversive to express concern about ▬▬▬▬▬, we plead guilty.
● If it is subversive to believe that there are better routes to peace than the ▬▬▬▬▬▬, we plead guilty.

● To PAGE 2

RESTRICTED

▲ The State of Emergency imposed press censorship. What words do you think have been blacked out on this newpaper's front page?

▲ (left) Hector Peterson, the first child to be shot dead by the police in Soweto on 16 June 1976.

political system of apartheid. Apartheid literally means 'apartness' of peoples with different colour skins; it is a philosophy which is based on difference and inequality. Consider the following facts and figures about South Africa under the apartheid system.

The South African government, which is almost exclusively in the hands of the whites, divides people into racial groups:

Africans	24	million
People of mixed race (coloured)	2.8	million
People of Asian origin	0.9	million
Whites	4.8	million

Africans, coloureds and Asians are often known collectively as blacks. Land is distributed as follows:

Whites	86.3%
Blacks	13.7%

Average monthly earnings in 1984, in rand (one rand was worth approximately fifty British pence in 1984),were as follows:

Africans	273
Coloureds	624
Asians	1,072
Whites	1,834

[1]

1
THE STRUGGLE FOR POWER
Early settlers

REMAINS OF ANCIENT POTTERY show that African Iron Age farmers lived in parts of South Africa as long ago as the fourth century AD. By the fifteenth century they were widely settled over the northern, central and south-eastern regions of modern South Africa. Along the East Coast lived the Nguni people, of the Zulu, Swazi and Xhosa chiefdoms. The Sotho peoples lived in the interior.

From the fifteenth century onwards, ships from Portugal, Holland and Britain began to sail around Africa as they established colonies in the eastern Spice Islands. 'The Cape of Good Hope', as the Portuguese named it, was an ideal watering place on the long voyage to India, and in 1652 the Dutch East

Early San rock paintings found in South Africa depict their struggle against animals and men and prove the existence of very early San settlements.

Dutch East India Company officials were not supposed to farm privately for their own profit. This picture shows an official who defied the ruling and used the Company's slaves to build his farm in the Cape.

. . . strongly insisted that we had been appropriating more and more of their land which had been theirs all these centuries, and on which they had been accustomed to let their cattle graze etc. They asked if they would be allowed to do such a thing supposing they went to Holland.[2]

India Company sent a group of its company servants to set up a refreshment station on the slopes of Table Mountain.

At the southernmost tip of South Africa lived the San (called Bushmen by later European settlers) who were hunter-gatherers, and the Khoi-khoi (whom the Dutch called 'Hottentots' because of a clicking sound in their language). The Khoi kept cattle, and the Dutch settlers, under their leader Jan van Riebeeck, bartered with them for meat, and used the land for growing vegetables. However, their differing attitudes to land and cattle soon led to conflict between the settlers, the Khoi and the San. Van Riebeeck records in his diary that the Khoi:

How do you suppose van Riebeeck reacted to this argument?

In these early confrontations the Dutch were the victors and eventually the San and Khoi were nearly wiped out by the military expeditions against them. The Khoi that remained were made slaves of the settlers, and slaves were sent from the Dutch East Indies. By 1700 a new social group had come into being – the offspring of the white settlers and their slaves, which in the nineteenth century became known as the 'coloured', or 'mixed race' people.

The British and the Boers

In 1815 possession of the Cape Colony, as the southern part of South Africa was then known, passed to the British after the Dutch were defeated in the Napoleonic wars. It was soon clear, however, that because of their different cultural and religious backgrounds the British and Dutch could not live together harmoniously and when the British abolished slave labour in 1834, on which Dutch farms depended, many Dutch farmers trekked into the interior looking for new land. The Boers (Dutch for farmers) saw themselves as the 'chosen people' of the Old Testament, born to inherit the 'promised land' of South Africa.

The Boers' 'Great Trek' of 1836–40 took advantage of recent large-scale warfare among the African chiefdoms of the interior. For the next twenty years the Boers and the British waged bitter wars of conquest against the independent chiefdoms and kingdoms of the interior. Eventually the Boers carved out two independent republics for themselves, the Orange Free State and the Transvaal, while the British expanded the Cape and took over Natal. African farmers then found themselves obliged to work on white farms in order to earn money to pay the taxes introduced by the British and Boer governments. In the British colonies anyone could vote who was literate, owned property, or earned a good salary – although in practice this meant very few blacks qualified to vote. In the two Boer Republics, blacks had no vote at all.

In 1867 diamonds were found in Kimberley, and whites flocked to diggings in South Africa from all over the world. Nineteen years later gold was discovered on the Witwatersrand in the Transvaal. Even more fortune seekers poured into South Africa, and a valuable mining economy developed, run by a group of fabulously wealthy and powerful men known as the Randlords, most of whom were British.

The new mining economy had a profound

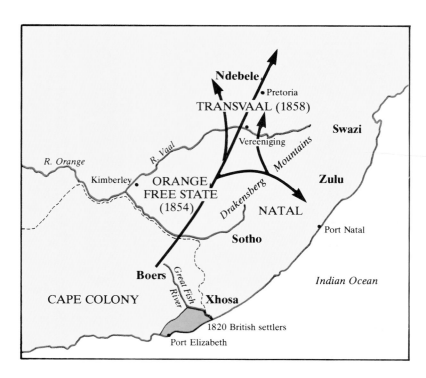

The path of the Great Trek, 1836–40, in which about 14,000 Boers are thought to have emigrated from the Cape Colony. The Boers disliked British rule for a number of reasons – competition over land, dislike of having to pay taxes and high rent, anger that English was made the official language – but particularly because British rule gave a measure of equality to non-whites.

effect on the lives of Africans, and also on relations between the British and the Boers. As a result of the rush for gold, by the early 1890s there were more 'uitlanders' (white foreigners) in the Boer Republics than Boers. Kruger, the Transvaal's President, wouldn't give these white foreigners the vote. His government charged enormous prices for the explosives needed for mining, and made the transport of gold as difficult and as expensive as possible for the mainly British mining magnates. Tension mounted and in the end war between the British and the Boers became inevitable.

Although the Anglo-Boer war (1899–1902) was officially a 'white man's war', blacks were extensively used as armed and unarmed workers by both the Boers and the British. Many blacks hoped that the land that they had lost would be restored to them if the British won the war. Why should they have had higher hopes of the British?

The British did indeed win the war, but at the 1902 Vereeniging peace agreement not only did they fail to restore their black supporters' land rights, but they agreed that the question of the African vote would be left to individual colonies to decide later. An opportunity to give the blacks rights in all the colonies had been lost, with crucial implications for the future.

In 1910 the British Parliament's Act of Union united the Boer and British colonies of the Cape Colony, Natal, the Transvaal and the Orange Free State under the leadership of the Boer war leaders, Louis Botha and Jan Smuts. Though the old voting laws were allowed to continue in the Cape, the vote was totally denied to blacks in the Transvaal and Orange Free State.

◀Boer gunners with a Krupp field piece during the Boer War, 1899–1902.

◀(above) A *Punch* cartoon shows the Rhodes Colossus straddling Africa. Cecil Rhodes became Prime Minister of Cape Colony in 1892. Does this cartoon present the British imperialist attitude favourably?

The Union of South Africa

By the 1910 Act of Union South Africa was to be governed by a parliament which met in Cape Town, although government administration was based in Pretoria and the Supreme Court in Bloemfontein. Britain retained nominal authority through a Governor-General, but in 1926 Prime Minister General Hertzog proclaimed his country's full independence, designing a new flag and appointing overseas ambassadors. Britain kept control of Basutoland, Bechuanaland and Swaziland, thus ensuring that there at least the lot of the African would not be wholly subservient to that of the whites.

The Boers (by now calling themselves Afrikaners) and the British did not live easily together. When the First World War (1914–18) broke out, many Afrikaners were sympathetic towards Germany. South African government policy, however, was to help Britain and her allies by invading the German colony of South West Africa (now called Namibia), but before this could be done Prime Minister Louis Botha had to put down a serious Afrikaner revolt at home. After the war South West Africa remained in South African hands as a League of Nations mandate.

In 1912 the South African Native National Congress (which became the African National Congress (ANC) in 1923) was founded by a group of chiefs, Christian ministers and intellectuals, as a reaction to the injustices brought about by the 1910 Union. These men belonged to the small élite group of Western-educated Africans who accepted that they had become part of a new colonial state. They believed all African people should see themselves as one nation rather than a collection of separate tribes, and they thought – mistakenly – that if they sent reasonable requests for the unjust laws to be changed, Britain and the white South African government would listen to them. Why do you think that it was important to the ANC that African people should not see themselves as belonging to tribes?

The ANC had very little success in achieving change, and in 1913 black rights were made considerably worse by the Natives' Land Act, which divided South Africa into

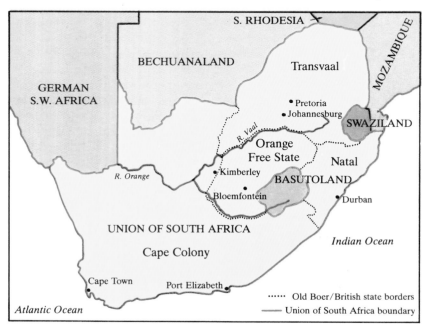

By the 1910 Act of Union, the four South African colonies – Cape Colony, the Transvaal, Natal and the Orange Free State – were united.

▼A commercial farmer and his labourers. By the 1913 Natives' Land Act, thousands of black Africans lost their land and were forced to work for the whites.

▲Early ANC leaders. In 1914 an ANC delegation visited Britain to put their protests about the pass laws and the robbery of African land to the British government and public.

exclusively black or white areas. It forced hundreds of thousands of Africans off farms they had either bought or were squatting on in the Transvaal and Orange Free State. Tenants and squatters who remained became servants of the whites. In 1922 General Hertzog's Afrikaner National Party, which demanded limitation to black rights, came to power. The National Party set about passing a series of Acts that turned racial discrimination into law. The Acts were designed to control the ever-increasing numbers of Africans who were moving into 'white' areas. The 1923 Urban Areas Act, for example, ruled that blacks should live in separate areas from whites.

The 'black peril'

From 1934 onwards, the white National Party, under the leadership of Dr D. F. Malan, made a concerted effort to unite the Afrikaners behind them. Since this group were a majority of the voters, Malan correctly surmised that with their support he could take power and hold it indefinitely. By 1938 they held twenty-seven parliamentary seats. But what really helped them was the outbreak of the Second World War.

Many Afrikaners found that their sympathies lay more with the Germans than with their old enemy, the British. As in 1914, however, Smuts' government fought with the Allies against Germany, but there was sabotage within South Africa by right wing groups, and in the 1943 election Malan's National Party won forty-three seats. Smuts' United Party was increasingly seen by the Afrikaners as weak and dangerously liberal.

With many of South Africa's white adult male population fighting in North Africa, thousands of poverty-stricken blacks from the reserves poured into the cities to work in the busy factories. It was difficult for Africans to find anywhere to live in 'white' areas. For the first time blacks were allowed to work in semi-skilled positions. Why do you think squatting and the crime rate soared during this period? Many whites began to feel they would be swamped by blacks. The way was opening up for a government that would nip the *swart gevaar* (Afrikaans for 'black peril') in the bud by making laws that would keep the blacks well and truly separate from the whites.

Dr D. F. Malan became prime minister in 1948. The National Party has remained in office ever since.

12

▲ Troops attempting to drive striking mine-workers back into the mines in the Witwatersrand, 1946.

▼Miners working underground. The whites' need to control black labour to work the mines has played a vital role in South Africa's political development.

After the war, unrest in the mines among low-paid black mineworkers led to a full-scale investigation of wages and conditions. The mining companies' conclusion was that:

> Families of African workers could be supported by agriculture in the reserves. Therefore African wages were no more than pocket money and need not be raised in line with the cost of living.[3]

This caused 70,000 black miners to go on a strike which brought the entire Witwatersrand gold-mining industry to a halt. The Smuts government called in the army, and nine miners were killed.

2

THE ADVENT OF APARTHEID
Nationalist victory – 1948

The Reservation of Separate Amenities Act led to such arrangements as these separate entrances for 'bantus' and whites.

IN PREPARATION FOR the 1948 election, the National Party under the leadership of Dr. D. F. Malan coined the word 'apartheid' as an election slogan, and the idea of racial separation was formally declared in the Party Manifesto: 'National policy must be so designed that it advances the ideal of ultimate separation on a natural basis.' The Dutch Reformed Church (the largest Afrikaans church) supported this view:

> *God divided humanity into races, languages and nations. Differences are not only willed by God, but perpetuated by Him . . . Those who are culturally and spiritually advanced have a mission to leadership and protection of the less advanced . . .*[4]

Do you believe that the Bible puts forward such views? Why was church support useful for the Nationalists?

The National Party won the 1948 election, with a slender majority over Smuts' United Party. From this time onward the policy of apartheid was gradually introduced. One historian has claimed that apartheid 'is really an abstract principle rather than a definite policy'[5].

The Population Registration Act of 1950 classified people as 'whites', 'coloureds' or 'natives'. There had to be a clear way, however, of determining a person's race. There were curious ways of proving that some white-skinned people were, in fact, black. If a comb could not pass easily through the 'try-for-white's' hair, they were considered to have black forefathers, and therefore must be registered 'coloured'.

To preserve the separateness of each group, the Prohibition of Mixed Marriages Act (1949) was passed, outlawing marriages between members of the different classified races, and a year later the Immorality Act made sex between whites and non-whites illegal.

Once everyone had been assigned a race, they had to be given separate areas to live in. The Group Areas Act of 1950, one of the cornerstones of apartheid, proclaimed 'specified' areas which could be occupied only by people of a particular racial group. As a result, entire black and coloured populations were moved to townships outside the cities when their traditional areas were re-zoned for whites. The 1953 Reservation of Separate Amenities Act made it a punishable offence for blacks to mix with whites on public properties such as parks, trains, swimming pools, beaches. Separate facilities were to be provided for all races.

What effect were these Acts intended to have on South African society?

SOUTHERN EDITION

GUARDIAN

Fourteenth Year No. 3. Registered at the G.P.O. as a Newspaper. PRICE **2d.**
THE GUARDIAN, THURSDAY, MARCH 9, 1950

He's Waking Up, Little Men, What Now?

▲ What is this cartoon saying about the South African government's attempts to 'control' black strength?

▼ Under which Act were these Indian-owned shops in a Johannesburg suburb due to be pulled down?

Migrant Labour

Ever since gold and diamonds had been discovered in the nineteenth century, ruling white governments had tried to ensure that blacks were only a temporary work force in white areas. Restrictions on where black people could live and travel became one of the pillars of the apartheid system. To understand why Acts were passed by the new Nationalist government to control the movement of black people from one place to another, these Acts must be seen in the context of the mining industry.

The Witwatersrand is the world's largest single source of gold. Huge numbers of labourers are required to work in these mines because much of the gold is situated over a kilometre underground and the ore is very low-grade. The lower the wages of the workers, the greater the profit for the mining companies. In the early years of this century many blacks could no longer support themselves through subsistence farming because their land had been taken by whites, so they had no real alternative but to work in the mines.

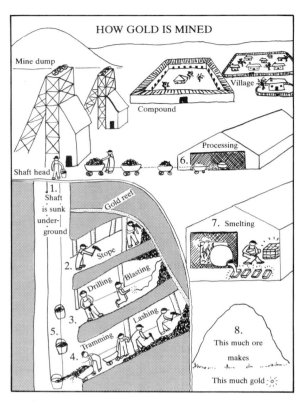

HOW GOLD IS MINED

Mine dump

Village

Compound

Processing

Shaft head

1. Shaft is sunk underground

Gold reef

2. Stope

Drilling / Blasting

3.

Lashing

5.

4. Tramming

6.

7. Smelting

8. This much ore makes

This much gold

▲ Huge numbers of labourers are required to work the gold mines.

◄ This view inside a compound for migrant mineworkers, reveals the cramped and uncomfortable conditions the men are forced to live in.

Because most black townships were some distance from the mines, a system of migrant labour came into being which still operates today. Many workers' contracts forced them to leave their families and to live in hostels near the mines. The following comment is by Mandlenkosi Makhoba, a migrant worker who works for a factory on the Witwatersrand:

> . . . for the sake of my family I was forced to leave my home . . . Vosloorus Hostel is one of the many badly kept hostels which are part of our lives. They are small and cramped for so many people. The hard stone floors are cold in winter. The rooms have no ceilings. They are hot in summer. And the hostels are far from town . . . I have worked hard for twenty years but have nothing in my hands.[6]

Why do you think the men are not allowed to bring their families with them?

To escape unbearable living conditions, many men broke their contracts and returned home. Towards the end of the nineteenth century pass laws were introduced, in order to prevent workers from moving from one job to another in search of better wages and conditions. Black people were made to carry documents saying in which area of the country they were supposed to be living and working. The Chamber of Mines Annual Report of 1899 stated that:

> The whole intention of the pass laws is to have a hold on the 'native' whom we have brought to the mines, be it from the East Coast, South or from the North, at considerable outlay to ourselves.[7]

What might have happened to the mining industry without the pass laws?

Here is part of a song that some black miners sing as they work. It addresses the white mining cities on the Witwatersrand.

(Egoli means Johannesburg.)

Benoni, Boksburg, Springs, Egoli,
we make you rich.
We hostel people make you rich.
You send us back home to die with empty pockets,
empty dreams and dust in our lungs,
chopped-off hands and your machines grinding in our brain.
Don't worry brother,
don't give up hope.
The sun shall rise for the workers.[8]

For years miners were not allowed to do skilled, better-paid jobs. Until 1986 the Mines and Works Act prevented blacks from qualifying for blasting certificates which would have enabled them to do skilled work.

Pass Laws

In 1952 the control of movement of black labour into white areas was considerably tightened by a series of influx control laws. The confusingly named Abolition of Passes Act forced all Africans to carry a single pass or reference book instead of a number of documents. Now no black could remain in a white area (including townships on the edges of white cities, like Soweto, Langa and Guguletu) for more than seventy-two hours. The only exceptions were outlined under Section 10 (1) of the 1945 Black (Urban Areas) Consolidation Act. The person concerned had to prove that he or she:

a   had resided there continuously since birth, or

b   had worked there continuously for one employer for not less than ten years, or had resided there lawfully and continuously for not less than fifteen years and was employed there, or

c   was the wife, unmarried daughter or son under eighteen years of age of a black in one of the above categories who, after lawful entry, resided with him, or

d   had been granted special permission to be in the area.[9]

Do you think that it would be difficult for a poorly-educated African worker to prove exemption from the Pass Laws under Section 10? The lucky ones who fitted into categories a, b and c were known as 'Section Tenners'. Those who came under category d were contract labourers, who were allowed in white areas for one year at a time.

Any authorized officer could at any time order an African to produce his or her reference book. Failure to comply could result in a fine or imprisonment. A pass book had to

An officer examining a pass book.

▲Women protesting against the government's decision to make them carry passes, in 1955.

▶A poster illustrating opposition to the pass laws.

show a person's ethnic group or race, employer, and present address. If it was correctly stamped and up-to-date, the holder could be present in a 'white' area on a temporary basis. By 1982, it was estimated that one person was arrested every two and a half minutes for pass offences.

Two laws were passed to force the removal from white areas of those Africans who were neither 'Section Tenners' nor migrant workers. First, the 1951 Prevention of Illegal Squatting Act gave the Minister of Native Affairs, Dr Verwoerd, powers to send 'illegal' African tenants to resettlement camps. What opportunities do you think this opened for abuse? Through the 1954 Resettlement of Natives Act the government could move not only the thousands of black squatters in white areas, but also whole, long-established communities. The era of forced removals had begun.

19

'Tribal homelands'

The pass laws were designed to ensure that all blacks (referred to as 'superfluous Bantu') whose labour was not required would remain in the 'tribal reserves'. The 1953 Bantu Authorities Act laid the foundations for these reserves to become 'independent' states. The idea was that 260 scattered 'tribal' areas would be consolidated into ten or so 'homelands', later to be known as 'bantustans', each populated by one particular tribe (for example, Zulu, Xhosa, Tswana). Chiefs were appointed by the South African government.

Nelson Mandela, a leading member of the African National Congress and outspoken

critic of apartheid in the 1950s, was critical of the Act. In an article entitled 'Verwoerd's Tribalism' he wrote:

> The Government have no intention of creating African areas which are genuinely self-supporting and which could therefore create a genuine possibility for self-government. If such areas were indeed self-supporting, where would the Chamber of Mines and the Nationalist farmers get their supplies of cheap labour?[10]

Why do you think the South African government encouraged tribalism in the creation of the homelands?

In the 1960s, under the title of 'separate development' rather than apartheid, the

The creation of the black 'homelands' was Verwoerd's plan for a permanent, 'respectable' segregation of blacks and whites.

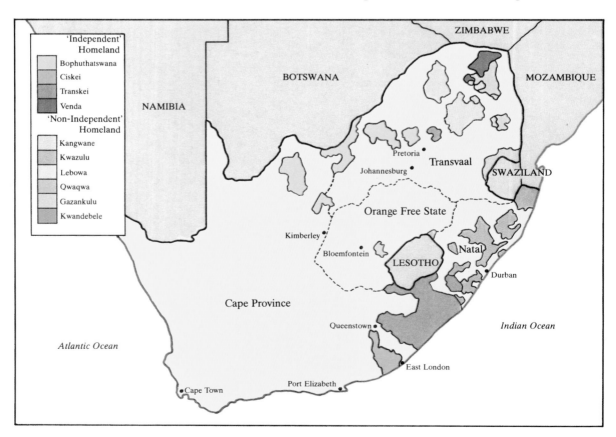

government pushed ahead with bantustan policy. Consider this remark by the Chairman of the Bantu Affairs Commission in 1968:

> *The Government's policy is therefore not a policy of discrimination on the ground of race or colour, but a policy of differentiation on the ground of nationhood of different nations, granting to each self-determination within the borders of their homeland – hence this policy of separate development.*[11]

Was the government's distinction between 'discrimination' and 'differentiation' a valid one?

Even though these homelands were too small and arid to support even half the black population, they were gradually to be given some form of independence in an attempt to show the outside world that 'separate development' could work. The idea was that South Africa would be broken up into a white state and a number of quite separate black states which would, it was hoped, become members of the United Nations.

The homelands depended entirely on South Africa for financial support. Most of the South African money that was allocated went on building townships to provide somewhere to live for the huge populations being forced out of 'white' South Africa into the barren and overcrowded land. Industries were established on the borders of some homelands so that black workers could commute across the border each day. However border industries do not provide enough work to solve the high unemployment problem in the bantustans. Why were the industries not established within the bantustans?

The effect of this forced removal to the homelands on the lives of Africans was enormous. Africans who had been cattle farming for generations in white areas that were now forbidden to them were forced to sell their livestock. Many lived in resettlement

A woman protesting in Johannesburg against the poverty of rural areas. Forced removal to the homelands meant many blacks lost land and livestock.

camps, erected for dispossessed Africans to stay in before moving to their designated bantustan. The camps were set in bleak stretches of land, hundreds of kilometres away from towns. The absence of facilities like running water, fertile land and adequate shelter caused disease and malnutrition.

Altogether between one and three million Africans were moved into the bantustans during the early 1960s. It was not long before large numbers of hungry women illegally began to leave the homelands to be with their husbands who were working in the white areas.

21

Education

A classroom in a bantustan school. Overcrowding and lack of basic equipment (such as chairs and tables) is still a common problem.

The Nationalist government claimed to be attempting to interpret God's will concerning the education of blacks. The ideals of the Institute for Christian National Education (CNE) stated:

> *The task of white South Africa to Christianise the native and help him on culturally has already found its closer focus in the principles of trusteeship, non-equality and segregation. Hence native education must be grounded in the life- and world-view of the whites, more especially the Boer nation as the senior white trustee of the native . . . (1948)[12]*

Although this passage is a little complicated, it gives a good insight into Afrikaner thinking. It is too easy to simply label the Nationalists as bad, and out for their own ends; many whites genuinely believed that they had a mission to 'Christianize' the Africans through their 'trusteeship'. Their feelings of superiority were misguided, but many did not consciously see themselves as exploiting the blacks. The fault was in confusing their own technological superiority with moral supremacy.

A specially-appointed commission recommended that the different races should receive different types of education. African children should be taught in their own 'tribal' or 'ethnic' language, and both English and Afrikaans should be taught:

. . . in such a way that the Bantu child will be able to find his way in European communities; to follow oral or written instruction; and to carry on a simple conversation with Europeans about his work and other subjects of common interest.[13]

There is no place for the Bantu in the European community above certain forms of labour . . . For that reason it is of no avail for him to receive a training which has as its aim absorption in the European community.[14]

The habit of doing manual work should be encouraged. What assumptions does this make about the position of blacks in the workplace? African education would not be compulsory and, although it would be run by the government's Department of Bantu Education, blacks would have to pay for it themselves, unlike whites whose schooling was free.

These recommendations were made law through the Bantu Education Act (1953). When he presented it, Dr Verwoerd, the Minister for Bantu Affairs, said:

Referring to the mission schools which had offered blacks the same education as whites, and whose subsidies the state now withdrew, Verwoerd continued:

Until now he has been subject to a school system which drew him away from his own community and misled him by showing him the green pastures of European society in which he is not allowed to graze.[15]

How did the Bantu Education Act further the National Party's goal of non-equality between blacks and whites?

The ANC responded to the Education Act with a boycott of government-controlled schools, and set up its own schools. This scheme collapsed when the government declared unlicensed schools illegal.

With public demonstrations threatened by police intimidation, some blacks showed their anger at their inferior education by daubing walls with slogans.

Trade unions

One of the few ways that industrial workers can improve their lot is by organizing themselves into unions. The individual labourer is powerless before an employer, but a workforce speaking with one voice – even striking if necessary – has immense bargaining power. For this reason, the South African government authorities have been quick to clamp down on black union activity.

In 1946 the Transvaal Chamber of Mines reacted to the miners' strike with this statement:

It is the opinion of the Gold Mining Industry that trade unionism is against the best interests of tribal Natives employed on the mines. They are not yet sufficiently advanced for trade unionism, nor do they themselves want it . . . it follows that the control of such unions would fall, inevitably, to persons not connected with the Industry . . . It is clear that the union is connected with and has the support of communistic influences.[16]

The Suppression of Communism Act, passed in 1950, allowed people who were named as communists to be banned from political organizations or restricted to particular areas in South Africa. According to the Act, 'communism' could mean:

- Any doctrine or scheme which aims at bringing about social or economic changes by the promotion of disorder.

or

- Any doctrine or scheme which aims at the encouragement of feelings of hostility between the European and non-European races of the Union.

Do you think that this is an accurate definition of communism as you understand the word? Why do you think that the government wanted the definition to be so broad?

SACTU organizers address workers outside a factory in the 1950s. Management would not allow workers to have contact with trade unionists.

◀Job reservation in a supermarket: a white cashier and a black packer. The cashier's job was for whites only.

▼Members of the white women's civil rights group 'Black Sash' protest against job reservation in the centre of Cape Town.

In 1953 there were over thirty unions for Africans only. That year, their powers were drastically cut by the Native Labour (Settlement of Disputes) Act which prohibited any strike action by Africans under any circumstances. Africans could not remain members of registered racially mixed unions. Unions for Africans could not link up with any political group, nor could they bargain over wages. Members could be arrested if they went on strike.

'Job reservation' was made official in 1956. The Industrial Conciliation Act made it possible for the government to restrict certain work to particular racial groups. These job reservations covered most industries: transport, the wholesale meat trade, road construction, lift operators and barmen in white public bars. In Cape Town, only whites could be ambulance drivers, firemen, or traffic policemen above the rank of constable. Can you see how job reservation went hand-in-hand with the Bantu Education Act?

In 1956 the non-racial South African Congress of Trade Unions (SACTU) was created. Its aim was to ensure that all African workers were organized into unions. By the 1960s SACTU was arguing that the unions

could not succeed without political change. Led by the African National Congress, SACTU threw itself into the struggle against the National Government. Do you think that unions were bound to become political?

RESISTANCE AND REPRESSION
Black resistance

OPPOSITION TO THE National Government and its apartheid policies came from all over the world, although governments disagreed over the best tactics to adopt towards the South African regime. Within South Africa resistance among the blacks centred around the African National Congress (ANC), the anti-apartheid Labour Party and the white liberal Progressive Party. Resistance was both passive, in the style of the great Indian leader Mahatma Gandhi, and violent.

The ANC was initially a moderate and pacifist organization which believed that reasonable requests to the white government would be given due consideration. In the 1940s a number of young men and women, including Nelson Mandela, Walter Sisulu, and Oliver Tambo, helped found the militant Youth League of the ANC. At the 1949 ANC conference, Mandela and his colleagues pushed through a 'Programme of Action' that was designed to abolish racial

A poster illustrating one of the key clauses of the Freedom Charter, adopted at the Congress of the People, 26 June 1955.

Police attacking women protesting in Durban, 1959. Is there any justification for such violence? After the Sharpeville massacre in 1960 the ANC and PAC were banned, and black opposition turned from non-violent to violent resistance. Can violence ever be justified?

discrimination through boycotts, strikes and civil disobedience. In 1951 the African and Indian congresses joined together to organize the Defiance Campaign which would use passive resistance to apartheid laws. Volunteers openly broke segregation laws, inviting arrest; protesters went to jail in their hundreds, and ANC membership soared. The government took stern action. Leaders of the campaign were arrested and charged under the Suppression of Communism Act. Heavy penalties were laid on anyone influencing Africans to break laws, and the campaign eventually collapsed.

Albert Luthuli, who was later awarded the Nobel Peace Prize, became President of the ANC in 1953. Under his leadership, a Bill of Rights which included *all* South African peoples, was discussed. Opponents of apartheid, including the ANC, the Indian Congress, the Coloured People's Organization, SACTU and the radical white Congress of Democrats met in Kliptown in 1955,

attended by about 3,000 delegates. This Congress Alliance drew up the famous Freedom Charter declaring that South Africa belonged to all its inhabitants, both black and white, calling for non-racial democracy, and equal opportunities in education and employment.

The government's response was to arrest 156 leading Congress delegates, including Nelson Mandela, and to charge them with treason. Their trial lasted four and a half years, but finally all were acquitted, as 'violent means' had not been used.

In 1959 a militant group of 'Africanists' left the ANC to form the Pan-Africanist Congress (PAC), led by Robert Sobukwe. In 1960 ANC and PAC protests ended in the tragedy of the Sharpeville shootings, after which both organizations were outlawed. The situation then became increasingly violent, the ANC and the PAC both established armed wings, Umkhonto we Sizwe (Spear of the Nation) and Poqo (we go alone), dedicated to meeting violence with violence and overthrowing the governing regime by force. These have been responsible for acts of violence and sabotage in South Africa. There have also been spontaneous outbreaks, as in Soweto in 1976 when 176 people were killed by police and 1,200 wounded.

The hero of black resistance was Nelson Mandela, imprisoned in 1962 on minor charges and then tried again for treason in 1963–4. His speech at his trial in 1964 has inspired his followers ever since:

During my lifetime I have dedicated myself to this struggle of the African people. I have fought against white domination and I have fought against black domination. I have cherished the idea of a democratic and free society in which all persons live together in harmony and with equal opportunities. It is an ideal which I hope to live for and achieve. But if needs be, it is an ideal for which I am prepared to die.[17]

Sharpeville

Defiant black demonstrators burn their pass books. This historic photograph was taken around the time of the Sharpeville massacre.

The PAC was established by members of the ANC who believed that only black Africans should make a stand against apartheid, and were suspicious of collaboration with sympathetic 'coloured', Indian or white groups, which they feared were dominating the Congress Alliance. They saw themselves as part of an Africa-wide movement towards independence. This split is a good example of the sort of problems that faced black resistance to apartheid. How do you imagine the South African government reacted to the split?

Both the ANC and PAC organized mass anti-pass campaigns for March 1960, and on 21 March Sobukwe and his followers deliberately broke pass laws. They were arrested, and Sobukwe was later sent to Robben Island security prison where he was to spend nine years. On the same day, huge crowds of Africans massed around Sharpeville police station, deliberately seeking

arrest by leaving their pass books at home. The police panicked, and opened fire. Here is a comment by Lt. Col. Pienaar, officer-in-charge that day:

> *I do not know how many people were shot. It all started when hordes of natives surrounded the police station. My car was struck by a stone. If they do these things they must learn their lesson the hard way.*[18]

What do the tone and the kind of language used by Pienaar suggest about police attitudes to black people?

There were 249 people shot at Sharpeville, mostly in the back; 69 of them were killed. Luthuli showed his support for both the PAC and the ANC by publicly burning his pass book. A national stay-at-home was declared in mourning for the dead. A young PAC leader, Philip Kgosane, led a crowd of 30,000 Africans deep into the heart of white

The dead and wounded outside Sharpeville police station, 21 March 1960, after the police opened fire on 3,000–5,000 African demonstrators.

Cape Town. Many of his followers were migrant workers who lived in the squalid bachelor hostels, separated from their wives and families in the Transkei. They returned to the Langa and Nyanga townships when Kgosane was promised an interview with the Minister of Justice; but when he arrived for the interview, Kgosane was arrested.

In an attempt to keep control of the volatile situation the government followed the massacre by declaring a nation-wide State of Emergency; 18,000 people were subsequently arrested, and on 8 April 1960 the ANC and PAC were banned. Political change by peaceful methods now seemed impossible.

The Sharpeville massacre drew the attention of people all over the world, maybe for the first time, to the sinister side of the policy of apartheid. Within weeks foreign companies withdrew £750 million of investment. Prime Minister Verwoerd, however, had little regard for the opinion of other nations, and he was keen to break links with the Commonwealth – he was planning a referendum among whites to decide whether South Africa should become a republic.

Repression

A refinery burning at Sasolburg, after being sabotaged by Umkhonto we Sizwe.

Soon after the Sharpeville massacre white South Africa voted to become a republic, and in 1961 South Africa left the Commonwealth. Johannes Vorster, who had been imprisoned for his pro-Nazi sabotage acts during the Second World War, was promoted to Minister of Justice. By this time Umkhonto we Sizwe were pursuing their sabotage plans with bomb explosions at power and transport installations. They attacked only 'hard targets' (buildings), and strenuously tried to avoid injuring people. Can the ANC and PAC be justified in turning to violent means to achieve change? In response to these attacks a number of repressive acts were passed, first by Verwoerd's government, and then by Vorster, after Verwoerd was murdered in 1966. These measures included:

- The banning of all public meetings.

- The 1961 Defence Act strengthening military training and police control.
- The 'Ninety Day Act' (1963) which enabled the police to arrest without a warrant anyone they suspected of being in any way involved with anti-government activities. People so arrested could be held for ninety days, and immediately re-arrested on release. In 1965 the period for which suspects could be held rose to 120 days, then to an unlimited time in 1966. Such detentions were made even easier in 1976 when a judge's permission was no longer required.
- The 1968 Publications Control Board. Despite this Board, the white press

remained essentially free until the 1980s.

- The Affected Organizations Act (1974) giving the South African Bureau of State Security (BOSS), answerable only to the prime minister, power to investigate and close down any suspicious organization, from a Christian society to a newspaper.

For a while, it appeared to the outside world that stability had been brought to South Africa by the new laws, and overseas capital from Britain and other European countries, the United States and Japan flooded back into the country. Massive reinvestment caused South Africa's gross domestic product to more than double from R5,349 million to R11,635 million. But how secure was South Africa's new-found stability? Section Six of the Terrorism Act, the most ruthless of the new security laws, allowed any police officer of or above the rank of lieutenant-colonel:

> . . . to detain for interrogation any person whom he has reason to believe is a terrorist or has information relating to terrorism for an unlimited period of time.[19]

What is a terrorist? What some call a terrorist others may call a freedom fighter. What do you understand by this? The Terrorism Act resulted in widespread torture of suspects, and the number of deaths in detention increased. Can a country be governed successfully for long by such repressive methods?

▲Police using a telephoto lens to snap and identify 'troublemakers'. What effect do you think this sort of surveillance has had on black South Africans' attitude to other white photographers?

◄Spot check. A white policeman stops in his patrol car to question two black people in Sharpeville.

Changes in labour

In the early 1970s, the needs of South African industry began to change. The country developed its own sophisticated electronics and engineering industries. The new technology meant that more skilled labour was needed than the white work-force could provide. Demand grew for black labour – with the result that blacks began to get more bargaining power. In 1973 a wave of massive strikes in Durban and on the Witwatersrand showed that black workers had remained effectively organized. Although the strike was put down and the army brought in, large pay increases were awarded.

These strikes proved to be a turning point in black trade union history. Vorster announced that, to satisfy the new demands of the economy, better educational opportunities must be given to people of all races. Why did the needs of an increasingly technological industry mean better education was needed for black people? For the first time the South African government had to recognize that blacks were going to be living in white areas on a permanent, not a temporary basis and the rigid system of job reservation was relaxed. Foreign pressure on South Africa, particularly the boycotting of sporting links with the country, also played an important part in the government's change of heart.

After the 1973 strikes, the government decided that it would be able to control African workers more effectively if they were allowed to form registered unions rather than organize illegally. Why should this be the case? Many trade union groups, like SACTU in the 1950s and 1960s, believed that real advances for black labour must be won through political activity. Other groups (known as 'workerists') considered that the

Police and strikers watch each other suspiciously in Durban, during the wave of massive strikes in 1973.

Thousands of black residents are evicted from their homes in Sophiatown near Johannesburg. This subsequently became an all-white area.

building of unions was the top priority, and that anything that endangered this aim should be resisted. What was the thinking behind this 'workerist' position?

Slowly, some of the most basic features of apartheid were being forced to change, simply to create a stable work-force. The government was beginning to re-examine the policy of migrant labour which split up families and caused tensions in the townships. At the Kimberley diamond mines, which had pioneered migrant labour and the closed compound system, miners from the homelands were now allowed to bring their families to live with them. In 1976 Africans living in white areas were allowed to obtain thirty-year leases on their homes in African townships. Yet despite these new trends, forced removals and resettlement continued to affect the lives of millions of black Africans.

After the official recognition of registered black trade unions industrial action was taken much more frequently and black wages increased. In 1971 the average white wage was nearly twenty-one times the average black wage, while by 1979 it was only seven times higher. The small gains of low-paid black workers were soon wiped out, however, by high inflation. During the seventies and eighties, many of the leaders and members of the new unions were banned, arrested or detained. Some have died in detention and it is clear that the path to full rights for black workers will be a steep and difficult one.

The students

A crowd gathered for Steve Biko's funeral procession. Biko died in detention on 12 September 1977. Five weeks later all Black Consciousness organizations were banned, although several groups still survive.

A new Africanist political movement, rooted in the banned Pan Africanist Congress, spread among young blacks during the early 1970s – Black Consciousness. The first aim of Black Consciousness was to conquer feelings of inferiority, and to develop a pride in black history. Steve Biko, the black student leader and founder-member of the South African Students Organization (SASO), opened the movement to all those who were discriminated against on grounds of colour and race, regardless of whether they were 'coloured', 'Indian' or 'African'.

The end of Portuguese colonial rule in neighbouring Angola and Mozambique in 1975 gave South African blacks new hope for their own freedom. SASO and the Black People's Convention (BPC) held rallies to celebrate the victory of Frelimo, the Marxist liberation movement in Mozambique, but these were broken up by police with dogs, batons and tear gas. SASO offices were raided, and student leaders were arrested under the Terrorism Act. After sixteen months of jail the nine accused were convicted as 'terrorists', for expressing the new attitudes of the Black Consciousness movement. Was this conviction appropriate for their crime?

It is interesting that the South African authorities maintained their insistence that all outspoken opponents of apartheid were 'terrorists', and all 'terrorists' were communist-backed. Two reasons for this are, firstly, that the Nationalist government is terrified of communism spreading among black Africans, and, secondly, because it knows that in a fight against communism it will be supported by conservative governments in Britain, the USA and Japan.

The influence of the Black Consciousness movement increased students' already great frustration at their inferior education, their inadequately trained teachers and the lack of books and equipment. When the Bantu Affairs Department (BAD) proposed that some subjects should be taught in Afrikaans, which was generally regarded as 'the language of the oppressor', students from Soweto rose in revolt. Why did they want to be taught only in English? On 16 June 1976, hundreds of schoolchildren staged demonstrations against the general injustices of Bantu education. They were met by armed forces and, to the horror of the rest of the world, hundreds were shot dead.

In the face of such brutal repression by police and army, students began to boycott their schools and destroy government buildings in the townships. Compulsory Afrikaans in schools was dropped and the government promised more funding for Bantu education, but many students regarded the government promises as hollow. Why do you think this was?

In 1977 all Black Consciousness organizations were banned. Steve Biko became the forty-sixth person to die in police custody, having suffered assaults which had caused fatal brain damage. Many have died in police detention before and since Steve Biko. What does the following poem by Christopher van Wyk suggest about official reasons for deaths in detention?

In Detention

He fell from the ninth floor
He hanged himself
He slipped on a piece of soap while washing
He hanged himself
He slipped on a piece of soap while washing
He fell from the ninth floor
He hanged himself while washing
He slipped from the ninth floor
He hung from the ninth floor
He slipped on the ninth floor while washing
He fell from a piece of soap while slipping
He hung from the ninth floor
He washed from the ninth floor while slipping
He hung from a piece of soap while washing [20]

After Soweto, protests and school boycotts spread across South Africa, much of it led by schoolchildren.

The opposition

It is very easy to over-simplify the troubles in South Africa. The problem is not a clear-cut black versus white situation. The blacks themselves are frequently divided as to the correct tactics to use to win greater freedom. Some, such as Chief Buthelezi of the Zulus, feel that they can get more for their people by a degree of co-operation with the white government. This, they feel, will win white respect for the blacks, enabling them to be seen as less of a threat, and so lead to greater understanding between the races. Others, like Archbishop Desmond Tutu, support non-violent action and call for the rest of the world to impose economic sanctions on South Africa. Yet others pursue a violent solution through acts of terrorism.

There is frequently tension between the blacks and the Asians, many of whom are quite successful businessmen, enjoying a higher standard of living than most blacks. The whites, too, are divided. Many have left South Africa; they have chosen to leave the country of their birth, their friends, and a high standard of living to start a new life elsewhere, rather than live in a country whose policies they feel to be morally wrong.

Other whites prefer to remain in South Africa and struggle to change the system from within. Their task has not been easy. With the death of General Smuts in 1950 the opposition United Party lost its great leader. The opposition parties' share of the vote fell from fifty-nine per cent in 1948 to thirty per cent in 1977. In 1959 the United Party split, with thirteen liberals breaking away to form the Progressive Party. The most well-known of them was Helen Suzman, so often a lone

The neo-nazi emblems of Eugene Terreblanche's Afrikaner Resistance Movement (AWB) are prominent at this right wing rally. The AWB utterly reject Botha's reforms.

Helen Suzman, one of South Africa's longest-standing and most outspoken white critics of apartheid.

voice of moderation in the tempest of South African politics. The United Party dissolved in 1976, many of its Afrikaner supporters having moved to the National Party.

More worrying in recent years has been the growth of right wing parties. In 1966 the National Party had split between those who were prepared to abandon petty apartheid (such as separate queues for different races in post offices), but preserve the grand apartheid design, and those who saw apartheid, as conceived by Verwoerd, as not open to relaxation of any sort. The first faction, led by Albert Hertzog, son of General Hertzog (founder of the original National Party), formed a new right wing party – the Hersigtige National Party (HNP). The remaining faction, led by Andries Treurnicht, became the Conservative Party (CP). There are also groups openly fascist in dress and policy. Their racism is unflinching. Faced with this upsurge in right wing sentiment, the government is faced with a dilemma: should it strengthen itself by appealing to the new right, thus moving even further from the blacks and world opinion? Or should it turn to the liberals, thus risking losing power to right-wingers under whom violence might be the only solution to the country's problems?

4

FOREIGN RELATIONS
Neighbours

◄South Africa's neighbours. Since 1948 many African countries have gained independence and have majority (black) rule. South Africa stands out in resisting black political power.

► (top) Robert Mugabe (left) and Joshua Nkomo (right). In 1980 Mugabe became Prime Minister of Zimbabwe. Do you think Mugabe's Marxist-based ideas had anything to do with the fact that the South African government tried to resist his coming to power?

► (bottom) Boots by his side, an MPLA soldier lies dead in Angola after a battle with UNITA forces.

A GLANCE AT THE map above will show that South Africa has frontiers with many different states. In 1948 there were the three British Protectorates of Bechuanaland (now Botswana), Swaziland and Basutoland (now Lesotho). To the north-east were the Portuguese colony of Mozambique and the British colony of Southern Rhodesia (now Zimbabwe). In the west South Africa administered the ex-German colony of Namibia (formerly South West Africa) virtually as a fifth province of the Republic. This gave South Africa a northern frontier with a second Portuguese colony, Angola. Between 1948 and 1974 South Africa's relations with all these neighbours were to change dramatically.

Throughout Africa there blew a 'wind of change', and with it came independence to Northern Rhodesia (now Zambia) in 1964.

The white government of the British colony Southern Rhodesia, however, was determined not to give up its position of privilege and power. Britain insisted that the colony must work towards majority (in other words black) rule, and to avoid this the white Prime Minister Ian Smith declared Rhodesia's independence in 1965, without Britain's consent. Two African Nationalist movements, the Zimbabwe African National Union (ZANU) and the Zimbabwe African Peoples' Union (ZAPU) set up offices in exile, and opted for armed struggle against Ian Smith's white Unilateral Declaration of Independence (UDI) in 1966.

Namibia's vast supply of diamonds (they lie loose on the beaches which are therefore cordoned off from the public) and other minerals has made South Africa reluctant to part with so valuable a territory. In 1966 the

United Nations declared South Africa's occupation of Namibia to be illegal, and in the same year, the national liberation movement SWAPO (South West African People's Organization) stated: 'We have no alternative but to rise to arms and bring about our own liberation'.

Portugal had its own system of white supremacy both in Angola and in Mozambique, and it relied heavily on South Africa. In 1974, however, the dictatorship in Portugal collapsed, having a dramatic and widespread effect on southern Africa as the Portuguese pulled out. In Angola two main groups, the MPLA and UNITA, fought for independence. Cuban forces moved into Angola to help the Marxist-orientated MPLA defeat the UNITA forces backed by South African troops. In Mozambique, ninety per cent of the Portuguese population (which represented most of the skilled labour force) fled, and the country gained independence in 1975 under a government formed by the Marxist liberation movement, Frelimo. Frelimo strongly opposed the apartheid system, and after coming to power allowed ANC guerrillas to infiltrate both South Africa and Rhodesia across Mozambican borders. Robert Mugabe's ZANU forces also operated from Mozambique, while Joshua Nkomo's ZAPU had its bases in Zambia. Can you see why the collapse of the Portuguese colonial authority was a threat to the white South African government?

The three British Protectorates all gained independence during the 1960s. However, as they depended totally on South Africa for their economic survival (more than half the adult male population of Lesotho works on the South African mines) their new 'independence' was not seen as a threat to their more powerful neighbour.

Mozambique

With the collapse of the Portuguese Empire in 1974, South Africa's neighbours searched for ways to become less dependent on South Africa. Well over fifty per cent of the exports of these 'frontline' states were routed through South Africa's railways and ports, while Mozambique and Lesotho depended very heavily on the earnings sent back by their migrant labourers who worked in South Africa's gold and coal mines.

With the achievement of Zimbabwean independence in 1980 the nine countries nearest South Africa (Zimbabwe, Zambia, Botswana, Tanzania, Angola, Mozambique, Malawi, Lesotho and Swaziland) established the Southern African Development Co-ordination Conference (SADCC) with a view to encouraging economic co-operation and reducing dependence on South Africa. South Africa responded by engaging in a process known as destabilization, which meant making life as difficult as possible for its neighbouring states. This ranged from imposing huge transport tariffs on goods, to providing military assistance to anti-Marxist movements in Angola and Mozambique. Some people lay the blame for the devastation in Mozambique at the feet of the South African government. Decisions to destabilize or invade neighbouring countries were taken in secret by the Minister of Defence, Magnus Malan, often without reference to parliament.

Until 1984 President Samora Machel allowed Mozambique to be used as a launching pad for ANC attacks on South Africa. As a result South Africa attempted to overturn Machel's Marxist government by backing the Mozambique National Resistance Movement (MNR), also known as RENAMO. Road and rail links were sabotaged, and the Cabora Bassa hydro-electric power station and oil pipelines to Zimbabwe were frequently attacked. By 1984 the economy of Mozambique was shattered. Machel drew up a treaty with South Africa at Nkomati in which both countries agreed

A cartoon poster by the End Conscription Campaign. What is the basic reason it gives for opposing conscription?

that their land would not be used as bases for enemy forces. The ANC presence was removed from Mozambique, but South Africa continues to provide RENAMO with supplies. South Africa denied its role in the devastation of this country, made worse by the famine of 1983–4, in which 100,000 people died.

The South African Defence Force (SADF) obliges white school leavers to do two years' military service, after which they go into an active reserve known as the Citizen Force for twelve years. Many white students object strongly to this and face arrest in rejecting the call-up; in 1984 the End Conscription Campaign (ECC) was launched.

▲ On 3 August 1988, 143 white men in a number of South African cities made simultaneous declarations of their refusal to serve in the South African Defence Force. In doing so they risked arrest and imprisonment.

◄Mozambican children whose village was destroyed by South African-backed bandits, line up for food in a camp for displaced persons.

Conscripts are called upon to fight on the borders of neighbouring states, patrol the townships, and even occupy 'trouble spot' schools. In June 1988, Magnus Malan disclosed that the SADF has established fourteen temporary military bases in or near 'unrest areas' in black townships at a cost of 5.7 million rand. What are these 'unrest areas'? Do you think the presence of the SADF will bring peace to them?

Namibia

South Africa continues to occupy Namibia at the cost of about five million rand per day. Although a 'Transitional Government of National Unity' has been set up by Pretoria, supposedly in preparation for Namibian independence, SWAPO refuses to partake in this 'interim' government. Health, schooling and other facilities remain organized along racial lines, and only 6,000 Africans in the population of 1.6 million have completed secondary school. As in South Africa, members of the South African Defence Force have taken over many teaching roles in schools, in an attempt to gain the 'hearts and minds' of schoolchildren. The South African army creates bases near the schools to deter attacks on them by SWAPO soldiers.

Namibia's economic life is dominated by its mining industry, where all the major companies are foreign-owned. The multinational diamond company de Beers, linked to Anglo-American (who control eighty per cent of the world's diamond sales), crippled Namibia's major source of income by over-

A South African motorbike patrol in North Namibia, out to prevent SWAPO guerrillas from entering the country from Angola. Within seconds of spotting rebels the patrol swerve to a halt, guns ready.

mining and stockpiling diamonds in case of the advent of a Marxist government. The London-based Rio Tinto Zinc Company owns the largest open-cast uranium mine in the world, Rossing Mines, and sells uranium (essential for nuclear fuel) from Namibia. In doing this, the company defies a 1974 ruling that minerals may only be removed from the area with UN permission.

In trying to reach a settlement with South Africa over the Namibian issue, the UN proposed the Security Council Resolution 435, calling for the removal of South African troops from Namibia, and UN-supervized elections for independence. South Africa continually raised objections to the resolution, and in 1978, in the middle of negotiations over it, carried out the Kassinga raid in which 700 Namibian refugees in South

Angola were killed.

South Africa continues to give military support to the rebel movement UNITA, under its leader Jonas Savimbi, with the aim of undermining the Marxist MPLA government of Angola. There have been horrific cases of torture and killing of civilians in Angola and Namibia. There are reports of Namibian peasants who support SWAPO guerrillas having their villages bombed and their crops and livestock destroyed by the SADF. The impact of the war has been especially disastrous for the children of Namibia, many thousands of whom have died from hunger, malnutrition and bombings. When General Magnus Malan was forced to admit in October 1987 that SADF troops had invaded Angola, he claimed that the attacks were aimed only at ANC and SWAPO bases.

In August 1988 South Africa announced a cease-fire agreement with Angola and Cuba, reached with the help of the United States government which has long encouraged 'constructive engagement' or friendly dialogue between South Africa and its neighbours. With the agreement came the hope that the long and bloody conflict in Angola, so damaging to both sides, may be at an end.

Demonstrators against apartheid march through London, 28 June 1986. Notice the banners declaring support for SWAPO. The protesters called upon Margaret Thatcher to impose full economic sanctions against South Africa.

The West

In August 1985 US banks decided to cease loans to South Africa, as the result of a tremendous upsurge of anti-apartheid feeling in the USA. South Africa's boom economy of the 1960s and 1970s had already begun to take a downward turn in 1983, now it came close to collapse. The South African rand dropped to less than a third of its former value, and the government was forced to suspend payment of its $14 billion foreign debt. Gold, which had reached a value of $850 a fine ounce in 1980, had dropped to under the $400 mark in June 1982, and showed no sign of recovering. In June 1986, after the worst drought in living memory (1982–84), and the continued escalation of black unrest, President Botha extended the 1985 State of Emergency to include the whole of South Africa.

Apartheid became an election issue in the USA, and during 1987 over seventy US companies, such as General Motors and Kodak, withdrew from South Africa. Why do you think they withdrew? Despite this, Western investment in South Africa still totals nearly $30 billion and provides technology essential to the South African economy and military security. Britain accounts for some forty per cent of total overseas investment, more than the combined investment from the USA and West Germany. A United Nations arms embargo against South Africa has not prevented several Western countries from providing South Africa with illicit military supplies. South Africa points out that the embargo has spurred the development of a

Archbishop Desmond Tutu, winner of the Nobel Peace Prize in 1985, was the first black South African bishop. As Archbishop of Cape Town he is now head of the Anglican church in South Africa.

Unable to compete in international athletics as a South African, Zola Budd applied for, and was granted, British nationality. Many people regarded this as a breach of the Gleneagles agreement.

self-sufficient domestic arms industry. If this is true, do you think the embargo a wasted effort?

There has been mounting pressure from liberation movements and prominent church representatives for the West to disassociate itself from South Africa. At a meeting in October 1985 the Commonwealth heads of government agreed on a package of sanctions against South Africa. These sanctions were criticized by the British Prime Minister Margaret Thatcher as 'immoral'. The British government claims that sanctions would hurt South African blacks more than whites. Does the fact that 150,000 British jobs depend on the South African connection alter the force of this argument? Do you think Mrs Thatcher is right to reject sanctions as a means of combating apartheid? In South Africa several leading opponents of apartheid, such as Chief Buthelezi and Helen Suzman, are also opposed to sanctions. However, Archbishop Desmond Tutu, who won the Nobel Peace Prize in 1985 in recognition of his efforts to dismantle apartheid by peaceful means, made the following comments:

> The argument that the blacks would be the first to suffer may be true yet there are at least two rejoinders: a cynical one is, when did whites become so altruistic? After all, they have benefited from black misery engendered by low wages, migrant labour etc. for so long. The less cynical is that blacks would probably be ready to accept suffering that had a goal and a purpose and would therefore end, rather than continue suffering endlessly.[21]

What is the 'goal and purpose' to which Archbishop Tutu refers?

South Africa is barred from the Olympic Games and other world sporting events. The 1977 Gleneagles Agreement obliged the Commonwealth countries to 'discourage contact or competition by their nationals with sporting organizations, teams or sportsmen from South Africa'. The South African government claims that sport in South Africa is now completely integrated. Bearing in mind the terms of the Group Areas Act, can this really be true? Even if it is, do you think the sports boycott should be lifted?

45

5

THE CLOUDED FUTURE
Gestures towards reform

BEFORE RETIRING IN 1978, Vorster introduced a plan to give Indians and coloureds a voice in central government. These power-sharing proposals for a multi-racial government were vigorously opposed by the more right wing elements of the National Party. In 1978 P. W. Botha became South Africa's new prime minister. He insisted on going ahead with Vorster's plans for a tricameral (segregated three-chambered) parliament. Only white voters were consulted by referendum on the proposed new Constitution. The majority black population was not to be represented in the new

Pieter Botha, State President of South Africa.

parliament, and most coloured and Indian voters boycotted the 1984 and 1988 parliamentary elections. In 1984 under the new Constitution, P. W. Botha became State President, and his powers were vastly increased. Why were black Africans not represented in the new parliament?

Botha is now seen as the man who started softening basic apartheid with his 'reforms'. In 1985 he abolished the Immorality Act, which meant that people of different races could now intermarry, but still would not be able to live in white areas. The foundation stones of old-style apartheid, the Population Registration Act and the Group Areas Act, remained untouched.

In 1955 the Western Cape had been declared a 'coloured labour preference' area (meaning that jobs would be given to 'Cape Coloureds' in preference to Africans). Not a single house was built there for Africans between 1972–80. Families of migrant workers were not supposed to live together, but many wives did come to join their husbands in white urban areas. Squatting was the only alternative for these families, for they were not allowed to live in the small, already over-crowded townships available for the 'Section Tenners'. From the mid-1970s onwards vast squatter camps, often made up of little more than cardboard boxes and plastic bags, began to spread out from the black townships. By 1974 there were at least 90,000 people living in conditions of unbelievable squalor, a few kilometres from Cape Town's white luxury suburbs. Crossroads, near Cape Town, has become the most notorious of these squatter camps.

In 1984 Botha decided that all 'Section Tenners' living in Crossroads were to be moved to a massive new township for Africans being built at Khayelitsha, forty kilo-

►Crossroads – one of South Africa's squatter camps – where 20,000 people live in makeshift homes. The government's solution to this is to raze it to the ground and send the black inhabitants to a homeland 1,600 km away. Compare this to the picture below, showing the luxury available to whites in this Johannesburg hotel.

metres outside Cape Town. The 'coloured labour preference' policy was scrapped and ninety-nine-year leasehold rights were to be offered to 'legal' blacks living in Khayelitsha. Botha now realized that the pass laws could not control the flood of migrant workers into white areas, and in 1986 the pass laws were finally abolished. A policy of 'orderly urbanization' was introduced instead, which ensured tight control over black peoples' movements. Those blacks not needed for their cheap labour could thus still be forcibly removed from urban areas and white farms to be 'resettled' in distant bantustans. Although the government announced in February 1985 that forced removals would stop, the following year some 60,000 Africans were 'assisted' to move and the homes of 2,425 squatter families were torn down.

Although Botha has been hailed by many as a great reformer, committed to dismantling apartheid, support for his actions has been mixed. Right wing Afrikaners, predictably opposed to reform, have gained support. Some opponents of apartheid, blacks and whites, were glad to see apparent change. A great many people feel, however, that apartheid cannot be reformed in this way, but can only be dealt with by complete abolition.

Unrest and violence

During the 1980s, in the absence of the banned ANC and PAC, four main political movements developed among South Africa's black population: the United Democratic Front, the Azanian People's Organization, Inkatha and the Congress of South African Students.

On 20 August 1983 some 10,000 people gathered at Mitchells Plain near Cape Town to form the United Democratic Front (UDF). This umbrella organization is not a political party, but is made up of nearly 600 anti-apartheid organizations which came together in opposition to Botha's government. People of all races can be members, and there are close links with the ANC and the Freedom Charter.

Another main branch of black politics includes those who see themselves as 'Africanists' first, and reject support from white radicals. When all Black Consciousness organizations were banned in 1977, the Azanian People's Organization (AZAPO) absorbed those blacks who did not agree with the Freedom Charter. AZAPO maintains that apartheid and all forms of racism are reflections of oppression of the working class, and is critical of the ANC's 'middle class' leadership.

Both the UDF and AZAPO are united in their rejection of the Zulu-dominated organization Inkatha, led by Chief Mangosuthu Buthelezi. Both groups regard

In 1985, increasing violence and a near-revolutionary situation led to the government's declaration of a State of Emergency in some areas of South Africa. Is repression a reasonable response to violence?

Buthelezi as a puppet because he leads the black homeland, Kwazulu, set up by the white government. Rivalry between Inkatha 'war-lords' and UDF members has resulted in extensive violence between blacks.

The Congress of South African Students (COSAS), a black student group which demanded a non-racial education for all, had been active in organizing large-scale school boycotts since 1979. In 1984, the year of the new Constitution, COSAS and the trade union movement organized massive strikes and school boycotts. White shops in selected areas were boycotted, young black radicals known as 'comrades' attempted to take over the townships, and a number of black councillors and policemen were killed in an attempt to clear the townships of government agents or 'collaborators'. The aim was to make the townships ungovernable. Why do you think that blacks who co-operate with the white authorities are regarded as 'sell-outs'?

As a response to this near-revolutionary

Children jeering at troops. Over half of South Africa's population is under fifteen years old. Do you think apartheid will end during their lifetime?

situation, a State of Emergency was declared on 21 July 1985 in the Transvaal and Eastern Cape. COSAS was banned the following month, causing boycotts and rebellions to intensify all over South Africa.

There are several reasons for violence between the different black groups: to some extent fighting has tribal roots, and there are genuine differences of opinion, as between the UDF and Inkatha. Social and economic conditions are also claimed to have caused the outbreaks of violence resulting in hundreds of deaths since early 1987. For instance, an average of eleven people live in one- or two-roomed houses in Edendale, a black township near Pietermaritzburg, where much of the fighting has occurred. On average there is one bread-winner per fifteen people, earning about R200 (£50) per month.

Crisis in South Africa

Despite the presence of armed troops and police in townships, unrest continues.

In February 1988, seventeen organizations, most of them affiliates of the United Democratic Front or AZAPO, were banned or severely restricted in their activities. They included the Detainees Parents Support Committee, a major human rights monitoring and campaigning body; the National Education Crisis Committee, convened to draw together parents, teachers and pupils in their educational struggles; and a number of youth congresses, including the militant South African Youth Congress launched in 1987. The union federation COSATU could no longer participate in protests of any kind. Union militancy was further restricted by the Labour Relations Amendment Act which placed severe limitations on labour's ability to bargain collectively.

The only critics of apartheid who still enjoy a measure of freedom to speak are church leaders – such as Dr Allan Boesak, Frank Chikane and Archbishop Tutu, all of whom have rejected violence as a means of dismantling the apartheid system, although all non-violent possibilities have been made illegal. Why do these church leaders still enjoy some freedom?

In many ways South Africa stands at a crossroads in its history. We might try to list the areas of possible optimism for its future:

- Ceasefire in Angola.
- Some relaxation of petty apartheid.
- Efforts by the Nationalists to broaden the base of their support by giving some rights to Asians and coloureds.
- A tacit recognition by the government that a rigid homelands policy will not work.

But do these really offer any hope? Consider the following, less hopeful, signs in South Africa:

- Botha's 'Reforms' have increased support for right wing white groups opposed to all compromise.

- The continued resistance and violence of black groups committed to armed struggle.
- South Africa's growing economic independence, supported by continued investment from Britain and Japan.
- The State of Emergency declared in the late 1980s, imposing strict censorship and making it increasingly difficult for the rest of the world to find out what is going on in South Africa.
- International condemnation has tended only to strengthen the South African government's determination to pursue its own course.

But how can one evaluate a complex situation such as the one in South Africa, for which the evidence and opinions are so contradictory? What is Archbishop Tutu's attitude towards those who claim South Africa is changing, as revealed in the following extract:

Desmond Tutu addresses the thousands gathered in Hyde Park, London, on 17 July 1988, to mark Mandela's seventieth birthday.

Some aspects of 'petty' apartheid have now been relaxed – such as separate park benches and toilets.

Those who claim that there is change are almost always whites. Very few blacks say so. When someone has been choking you, he cannot tell you, 'Hey, things are better now, I am not choking you quite so hard.' . . . The world will believe only when we, the victims, say, 'Ya, things are changing at last.'[22]

Leading figures

Biko, Steve, 1946–1977

Went to Natal University in 1966 to study medicine; left the white-dominated National Union of Students to form the all-black South African Students Organization in 1969. A leading figure in the Black Consciousness movement, he formed the Black People's Convention, and several community-based organizations. In 1975 he was held in detention without trial for 137 days. Arrests and banning orders followed until he died of head injuries, while in custody, in September 1977.

Boesack, Allan, 1945–

President of the World Alliance of Reformed Churches. Helped found the United Democratic Front in 1983. A powerful spokesman against apartheid, he believes that the struggle against apartheid is also a struggle for the integrity of the Christian religion.

Botha, Pieter Willem, 1916–

Lifelong member of the National Party. Closely involved with implementation of the Group Areas Act. Minister of Defence 1965–78. Responsible for the South African Army's entry into Angola in 1975. Prime Minister of South Africa 1978–84, he committed the National Party to a programme of reform and change, including the extension of the vote to 'coloureds' and Indians in a new tricameral system of parliament, and became the first state president under the new Constitition in 1984.

Buthelezi, Mangosuthu Gatsha, 1928–

Born into Zulu royal family. Studied history at Fort Hare University. Member of the Youth League of ANC. Took up position as chief of the Buthelezi tribe in 1953 and was appointed chief minister of the KwaZulu 'homeland' in 1976. Founder of a movement

Buthelezi addressing an Inkatha rally.

Nelson Mandela, leader of the African National Congress, was imprisoned in 1962. He has remained a figurehead for black resistance to apartheid despite, or even because of, his long imprisonment.

known as Inkatha yeNkululeko ye Sizwe (Freedom of the Nation) which opposes apartheid and desires universal franchise but is prepared to accept alternatives to maintain peace in Southern Africa. Buthelezi is against sanctions and calls for increased foreign investment.

Malan, Magnus, 1930–

Received a military education at the University of Pretoria and subsequently served in the marines and in the army. Rose to become Chief of SADF in 1976. Worked closely with the then Defence Minister, P. W. Botha in

developing an overall military and political strategy to counter the attacks against apartheid coming from within and without South Africa. He became a National Party MP in 1981 and is currently Minister of Defence. Malan is widely expected to be the next leader of the National Party after P. W. Botha.

Mandela, Nelson, 1918–

Born into the royal family of the Tembu in the Transkei. Expelled from Fort Hare University in 1940 for involvement in student politics. Obtained a law degree through a correspondence course. Established the first

African law practice in Johannesburg with his partner, Oliver Tambo, in 1952. Together with Tambo and Walter Sisulu, Mandela founded the Youth League of the ANC and eventually became its national president. In 1952 he was arrested for leading the Defiance Campaign which deliberately broke apartheid laws. In 1956 Mandela was again arrested and charged with high treason. Four and half years later, he was acquitted. After the Sharpeville Massacre in 1960 Mandela helped to form the military wing of the ANC. He went into hiding and travelled abroad but was arrested again in 1962 and sentenced to five years imprisonment for illegally leaving the country. During this imprisonment the police produced new evidence against him and he was sentenced to life imprisonment in 1964 for 'sabotage' and for 'conspiracy to overthrow the government by revolution'. Although he was charged under the Suppression of Communism Act, Mandela made it clear at his trial that he was not a Marxist and that he was in favour of parliamentary democracy along British lines.

Mandela, Winnie, 1934–

Trained as a social worker and became South Africa's first black medical social worker. Married Nelson Mandela in 1958. Arrested in the same year for her part in the anti-pass campaign. Member of the Executive of the ANC Women's League until it was banned in 1960. Kept in solitary confinement under the Terrorism Act for seventeen months in 1969. Subsequently arrested several times for breaking banning orders. A founder member of the Black Parents Association founded after the Soweto demonstrations in 1976 to help children affected by police action.

Robert Sobukwe, the African nationalist leader, on Robben Island where he was imprisoned for many years.

Sisulu, Walter, 1912–

Born into a peasant family in the Transkei. After being sacked from a bakery for organizing a strike he became Treasurer of the ANC Youth League in 1940 and was elected Secretary-General of the ANC in 1949. Sisulu worked closely with the Indian Congress in campaigning against the race laws and in the early 1950s became an international figure speaking against apartheid all over the world. He stood trial with Mandela in 1956 and again at the Rivonia Trial where, like Mandela, he was sentenced to life imprisonment. Husband of Albertina Sisulu (president of the United Democratic Front in the Transvaal and president of the Federation of South African Women).

Sobukwe, Robert, 1924–78

Educated at Fort Hare University where he was an outstanding student of literature. Joined the ANC Youth League in 1948. Became a teacher but was dismissed from his post for speaking publicly in support of the Defiance Campaign in 1952. Appointed lecturer in African Studies at Witwatersrand University in 1954. A noted intellectual, he edited *The Africanist* and led a breakaway group from the ANC which formed itself into a new liberation movement – the Pan-Africanist Congress. Sobukwe was unanimously elected president of the PAC in 1958. In 1960, after organizing the Sharpeville anti-pass campaign, Sobukwe was arrested and spent the next nine years in prison. On his release he was offered numerous posts by American Universities but the government prevented him from leaving the country. He died in 1978.

Suzman, Helen, 1917–

After a career as a history lecturer she joined the United Party to campaign for the rights of Africans in urban areas and became a Member of Parliament in 1953. The United Party split over the issue of resettlement and Suzman helped to form the new Progressive Party which campaigned vigorously against the growth of apartheid legislation in the 1960s. From 1966–74 she was the only representative of the Progressive Party in parliament. She has twice been nominated for the Nobel Peace Prize.

Tambo, Oliver, 1917–

Educated at a Methodist Mission School and Fort Hare University. Taught science and maths at a secondary school in Johannesburg before studying law and setting up a legal practice with Nelson Mandela. He joined the ANC in 1944 and rose to become the secretary-general in 1955. A devout Christian, Tambo was about to be ordained as a priest when he was arrested in 1956 under charges of high treason which were later dropped. He was asked to leave the country by the ANC when the organization was banned in 1960 and he escaped from South Africa to Botswana. In 1965 Tambo set up a guerrilla training camp in Morogoro, Tanzania which subsequently became the military headquarters of the ANC. Following the death of Albert Luthuli in 1967 he became the acting-president of the ANC, a position which he still holds.

Tutu, Desmond, 1931–

Ordained as a priest in 1961, Tutu studied theology in London where he gained his Masters degree in 1966. He became Bishop of Lesotho in 1978 and was appointed secretary-general of the South African Council of Churches in the same year. He has been honoured world-wide for his determination in resisting apartheid peacefully, he supports the Free Mandela campaign and believes in peaceful civil disobedience. In 1985 he was awarded the Nobel Prize for Peace. He is now a powerful voice amongst those calling for economic sanctions against South Africa. He was Archbishop of Johannesburg until 1987, when he became Archbishop of Cape Town.

Verwoerd, Hendrik, 1901–66

Born in Holland. Known as one of the 'architects of apartheid' because he created the idea of the 'bantustan' and of 'bantu education'. Became vice-chairman of the National Party in the Transvaal in 1946, Minister of Native or Bantu Administration in 1950, and prime minister in 1958. He was assassinated in 1966.

Important dates

Events

Date	Southern Africa	Date	Rest of World
1964	Mass political trials with life sentences on Mandela, Sisulu and others.	1964	Malawi and Zambia (Northern Rhodesia) achieve independence. Tanganyika and Zanzibar unite to become Tanzania.
1966	Prime Minister Verwoerd is assassinated; J. B. Vorster becomes prime minister. United Nations declares South Africa's occupation of Namibia to be illegal.		
1967	Terrorism Act.		
1969	Steve Biko founds Black Consciousness-inspired South African Students Organization (SASO).		
1973	Major strikes organized by black workers in Durban and Witwatersrand.	1972	Ugandan Asians expelled, flee to UK.
1974	Collapse of Portuguese colonial empire in Mozambique and Angola.		
1975	Independence of Mozambique and Angola. South African troops invade Angola from Namibia.		
1976	Soweto students uprising.		
1977	Steve Biko dies in police detention. All Black Consciousness organizations are banned.		
1978	P. W. Botha becomes prime minister. Kassinga raid: South African armed forces kill 700 Namibian refugees in South Angola.	1979	Afghanistan invaded by USSR. Margaret Thatcher becomes first British woman prime minister.
1980	Umkhonto we Siswe sabotages Sasolburg oil refinery. Renewed waves of school boycotts and protests by black students.	1982	Argentina seizes Falkland Islands: Britain recaptures them in 10 weeks.
1983	United Democratic Front formed.		
1984	Indians and 'coloureds' brought into new tricameral system of parliament and new Constitution. Massive strikes, school boycotts, unrest in townships. Nkomati peace agreement between Mozambique and South Africa.		
1985	State of Emergency declared in parts of South Africa. COSAS banned; COSATU formed. Immorality Act abolished. Bishop Desmond Tutu wins Nobel Peace Prize.	1985	Mikhail Gorbachev becomes leader of USSR: era of *glasnost* (openness) begins.
1986	Pass laws abolished. Nation-wide State of Emergency declared.		
1987	Severe censorship restrictions imposed on media.		
1988	Seventeen anti-apartheid organizations banned or restricted in activities. Angolan ceasefire agreed.		

Glossary

Afrikaans	Official language of the Republic of South Africa, closely related to Dutch and Flemish.
Afrikaner	White native of the Republic of South Africa, descended from the Dutch settlers.
ANC	African National Congress, South Africa's oldest political party, founded in 1912, current president is Oliver Tambo. The ANC is banned by the South African government.
Apartheid	Literally means 'apartness'. Official government policy of the separation of races because of their colour.
Azania	Name used by AZAPO members as the one that will replace 'South Africa' in the event of black majority rule.
Bantu	A group of languages, from southern, eastern and central Africa. A term used by the South African government in the 1950s and 1960s to refer to black Africans. Considered by blacks to be a derogatory term.
Bantustan	Area reserved for black Africans to live in with a small amount of self-government. Their official name is homelands.
Boer	Literally means 'farmer' (from the Dutch). Used to describe white South Africans of mainly Dutch descent who are now known as Afrikaners. Boer is now rather derogatory.
Broederbond	A secret society of white Afrikaner Nationalists formed in 1918, open only to males who are totally Afrikaans, without any English connections.
Communism	A political and economic theory based on the ideas of Karl Marx, who believed in abolition of private property and the creation of a classless society.
Detention	Holding a person in prison without trial.
Embargo	A government ban on trade with another country.
Frelimo	*Frente de Libertacao de Mocambique,* Marxist liberation movement that came to power in Mozambique at the end of Portuguese rule in 1975.
Human rights	Certain rights all people should be allowed: for example liberty, justice, not to be tortured or imprisoned without a fair trial.
Inflation	Rise in prices and cost of living
Influx	Literally means flowing in. Influx control laws limit the movement of people into certain areas.
League of Nations mandate	A territory under the trusteeship of the League of Nations that is given to another country to administer, sometimes with the intention of preparing the territory for independence.
Marxist	Followers of the economic and political theory that class struggle is the way to achieve change, and that capitalism will ultimately be replaced by communism.
Media censorship	Controlling or suppressing what is written and broadcast in newspapers and on the television or radio; for example, reports which are politically unacceptable to the government.
Migrant labour	People who have to travel from a black homeland, or from outside South Africa, to their place of work in 'White South Africa' – where they have no political rights.
Militant	Aggressive and vigorous in the support of a cause, not necessarily using violence.

MPLA	*Movimento Popular de Libertacao de Angola.* Cuban-backed Marxist liberation movement which came to power in Angola at the end of Portuguese rule in 1975.
Pan-African	Belief that there should be political unity among all African countries.
Pass	A document dictating areas in which a person is, or is not, allowed to be.
Prohibit	To forbid by law.
Referendum	A general vote by the electorate taken to settle an important political question.
Repression	Keeping people under control by force and by use of heavy restrictions.
Sabotage	Deliberate destruction or damage.
Sanctions	Action taken by one state against another, as a penalty for their behaviour or form of government which goes against international law. For example, refusing to trade with South Africa, banning their athletes from international competition, withdrawing foreign investment.
Segregation	Separation of different races according to their colour.
State of Emergency	Set of regulations and restrictions to cope with a state of public disorder and unrest which is a threat to government control. Involves banning gatherings and mass funerals, sealing off areas, greater restrictions on movement, removal of people to other areas, press censorship, curfews and widespread detention.
SWAPO	South West Africa People's Organization is the main liberation organization in Namibia with headquarters in Lusaka, Zambia.
Trade union	Association of workers, formed to bargain with the employer to improve and protect their wages and working conditions.
UNITA	*Uniao Nacional para a Independencia Total de Angola.* Liberation organization which lost to MPLA in Angola in 1975 but (with South African support) has continued fighting a civil war ever since.
Workerist	Africans who believe that the greatest priority for black labour is building up trade unions, rather than political activity.

Further Reading

Text books

Cameron, T. and Spies, S. B. (eds.), *An Illustrated History of South Africa*, Jonathan Ball, Johannesburg, 1986.

Omer-Cooper, J. D., *History of Southern Africa*, James Currey, London, 1987.

Parsons, N., *A New History of Southern Africa*, Macmillan, London, 1982.

Shillington, K., History of Southern Africa, Longman, 1987.

Easier Books

Bray, Ian, *Chicualacuala: Life on the Front Line – a photographic report on Mozambique*, OXFAM, 1987.

Brittain, Victoria and Abdul Minty (eds.), *Children of Resistance – on children, repression and the law in apartheid South Africa*, Kliptown Books, London, 1988.

Callinicos, Luli, *A People's History of South Africa, Vol. 1 – Gold and Workers, 1886–1924, Vol. 2 – Working Life, 1886–1940*, Ravan Press, Johannesburg, 1981 and 1987.

Children Under Apartheid, International Defence and Aid Fund for Southern Africa, (IDAF) 1980.

Fighting Apartheid: A cartoon history, IDAF, 1988.

Frederikse, Julie, *South Africa: a different kind of war*, James Currey, London, 1986.

Gouwenius, Peder, *Power to the People! South Africa in Struggle: A Pictorial History*, Zed Press, 1981.

Harries, A., Brown A. and Diski R., *The Child is Not Dead: Youth Resistance in South Africa 1976–86*, BDAF/ILEA, 1987.

Harris, Sarah, *Timeline South Africa*, Dryad Press, 1988.

Herbstein, Denis, *White Man, We Want to Talk to You*, Andre Deutsch, 1979.

Leach, Graham, *South Africa*, Methuen Paperback, 1987.

Lipman, Beata, *We Make Freedom: Women in South Africa*, Pandora Press, 1984.

Naidoo, Beverley, *Censoring Reality: An Examination of Books on South Africa*, BDAF/ILEA, 1984.

This is Apartheid, IDAF, 1984.

What Is History? A new approach to history for students, workers and communities, Skotaville Education Division, Johannesburg, 1987.

Women Under Apartheid, IDAF, 1981.

Woods, Donald, *Biko*, Penguin, 1978.

Scholarly Works

Davenport, T. R., *South Africa, A Modern History*, Ravan Press, Johannesburg, 1986.

Hanlon, Joseph and Omond, Roger, *The Sanctions Handbook*, Penguin Special, 1987.

Hanlon, J., *Beggar Your Neighbours; apartheid power in Southern Africa*, James Currey, London, 1986.

Hirson, B., *Year of Fire, Year of Ash. The Soweto Revolt: Roots of a Revolution?*, Zed Press, London, 1979.

Lodge, T., *Black Politics in South Africa since 1945*, Longman, London, 1983.

Original Sources

Biko, Steve, *I Write What I Like*, Heinemann Educational Books, 1978.

Cries of Freedom – Women in Detention, Catholic Institute for International Relations (CIIR), 1988.

Joseph, Helen, *Side by Side: Autobiography*, Zed Press, 1986.

Luthuli, A., *Let My People Go: an Autobiography*, Fontana Books, 1963.

Mandela, Nelson, *No Easy Walk to Freedom*, Heinemann, London, 1973.

Mandela, Winnie, *A Part of My Soul: Autobiography*, (eds.) Anne Benjamin and Mary Benson, Penguin, 1985.

Plaatje, S. T., *Native Life in Southern Africa*, Longman, London, 1987.

Two Dogs and Freedom: Children of the Townships Speak Out, Ravan Press, Johannesburg, 1986.

Notes on sources

1 *Profile: South Africa*, Catholic Institute for International Relations, 1986.
2 Thomas, H. B. (ed.), *Journal of Van Riebeeck Vol. 1 1661–1655*, Cape Town, Balkana, 1912.
3 Lansdown Commission, 1943–46.
4 Commission of the Dutch Reformed Church, 1950.
5 Danziger, C., *A History of Southern Africa*, Oxford, 1983.
6 Makhoba, Mandlenkosi, *The Sun Shall Rise for the Workers*, Ravan Press, Johannesburg, 1984.
7 Chamber of Mines Annual Report, 1899.
8 Makhoba, Mandlenkosi, *op. cit.*
9 Section 10 (1) of the Black (Urban Areas) Act, as amended by the Bantu Laws Amendment Act of 1964.
10 Mandela, Nelson. *Verwoerd's Tribalism*, Liberation, May 1959.
11 Bantu Affairs Commission, 1968.
12 Manifesto of the Institute for Christian National Education, February 1948.
13 Eiselen Commission, 1949.
14 Dr H. Verwoerd speaking in the South African Senate, 7 June 1954.
15 *Ibid.*
16 Official statement by the Gold Producers' Committee of the Transvaal Chamber of Mines, 1946.
17 Mandela's statement from the dock in Pretoria Supreme Court at the opening of the defence case, 20 April 1964.
18 *Daily Herald*, London, March 1922.
19 Section 6 of the Terrorism Act, 1967.
20 Christopher van Wyk, *Poets to the People: South African Freedom Poems*, ed. Barry Feinberg, Heinemann Educational Books, 1980.
21 Archbishop Tutu, *Profile: South Africa, op. cit.*
22 From a speech delivered by Bishop Tutu at the University of Witswatersrand, Johannesburg, 14 September 1985, taken from *Apartheid in Crisis*, ed. Mark A. Uhlig, Penguin Books, 1986.

Acknowledgements

The author and publishers would like to thank the following for allowing their illustrations to be reproduced in this book: Camera Press 9 (bottom), 12, 15 (bottom), 23, 28, 31 (top and bottom), 33, 35, 37, 39 (bottom), 42, 44, 47 (right), 51 (top), 53; IDAF cover, 4, 5 (left and right), 6, 7, 11 (top and bottom), 13 (top and bottom), 15 (top), 16, 17, 18, 19 (top and bottom), 21, 22, 24, 25 (top and bottom), 26, 27, 32, 34, 40, 41 (top and bottom), 49, 52; Popperfoto 29, 39 (top), 43, 45, 51 (bottom), 54; Punch 9 (top). The maps were supplied by Jenny Hughes.

While every effort has been made to secure permission, in some cases it has proved impossible to trace the copyright holders. The publishers apologise for this apparent negligence.

Index